T0061118

Broad Stripes *and* Bright Stars

PIONEER EDITION

By Peter Winkler

CONTENTS

Broad Stripes and Bright Stars

BY PETER WINKLER

It is bright. It is bold. And it is the United States' most powerful symbol—the American flag.

Car after car pulled up to the stadium. It was September 15, 2001. It was a hot day in Arizona. People piled out of their cars. They came in red, white, and blue T-shirts.

The United States had been attacked four days before. Many people had died. The people in Arizona wanted to show their love of their country. They made a huge "human flag."

MAKING THE FLAG

People in red shirts formed stripes. So did most people wearing white. Blue shirts became a background for white stars. It took two hours to make the flag. Then it was time for a picture.

A photographer snapped photos from a helicopter. One became a poster. It helped raise almost $400,000. The money went to the families of people who had been killed.

United They Stood.
People in Arizona made this "human flag."

Changing Nation
Changing Flag

The first U.S. flag had 13 stars and stripes—one for each state. Originally, each new state got a stripe and a star. But that got messy. So Congress stuck with just 13 stripes.

1777 *(13 stars and 13 stripes)*   **1795** *(15 stars and 15 strip*

RAISING THE FLAG

The "human flag" was a way to raise money. But that is not all. The flag was also a **symbol,** or sign. One person said the flag showed that "we are all Americans and we are all one big family."

Millions of other people also flew **Old Glory** after September 11. Some painted the flag on walls and lawns. Drivers pasted it on car bumpers. Store owners put it in windows. Eight out of every ten Americans were displaying a flag.

RED, WHITE, AND WHO?

Americans love their flag. It has always been the nation's most powerful symbol. Yet many people know little about its history.

For example, do you know who designed the first flag? Most people think Betsy Ross did. But she did not. In fact, no one knows for sure who designed it.

▼ **Going Places, Sticking Around.**
CAR: Paint and patriotism in Maryland create a roadside salute to America. *STAMP:* This special stamp was issued in October 2001.

FIRST FLAG

We do know one thing. The design of the first flag was chosen on June 14, 1777.

Who chose the design? People in the **Continental Congress.** That was the first government of the United States. Members said the flag should have 13 red and white stripes. It should have 13 stars. Each star and stripe stood for a state.

THE CHANGING FLAG

Over time, the United States changed. Its flag did too. The first change came in 1795. Kentucky and Vermont had become states. So Americans added two stars and two stripes to the flag.

(20 stars and 13 stripes)   **1876** (37 stars)   **1912** (48 stars)   **1960** (50 stars)

Old Glory, Young Hope.
This Nevada scene warmed Americans' hearts during the sad days of 2001. "Don't give up," it seemed to say. "Today hurts. But tomorrow can be bright as a child's eyes and wide–open as her arms."

5

A SPECIAL SALUTE

★★★★★★★★★★★★★

WORLD WAR II

On December 7, 1941, Japan bombed Pearl Harbor in Hawaii. The United States declared war the next day. The following Fourth of July, hundreds of U.S. magazines worked together to boost patriotism.

Each put the Red, White, and Blue on its cover. From *Aviation* to *Master Comics* to *Vogue*, Americans saw Old Glory everywhere. Those patriotic magazines included NATIONAL GEOGRAPHIC. It had never before used a picture on its cover.

Nearly a hundred flag covers from 1942 are on display at the National Museum of American History in Washington, D.C.

A LAW FOR FLAGS

More states came along after 1795. People tried adding even more stripes to the flag. It looked awful. So **Congress** made a law in 1818. The flag would have only 13 stripes. But each state would get a star.

WORDWISE

Congress: part of the U.S. government from 1789 to present

Continental Congress: first government of the United States, lasting from 1774 to 1789

Old Glory: nickname for the U.S. flag first used by Capt. William Driver in 1831

symbol: sign that stands for something

MARK THIESSEN

SEEING STARS

The 1818 law did not say how the stars should look. Most flag makers put them in rows. Others put them in circles or X-shapes.

In 1912, the United States made a new rule. The stars must be in straight rows. There were 48 stars at the time.

Then came two new states. Alaska joined in 1959. Hawaii did so a year later. So the flag got a new look. It had 50 stars. That is the flag that the country still uses today.

The flag has changed in many ways since 1777. Yet its power has stayed the same. The flag is still a symbol of our country and its people.

Symbols U.S.A.

Suppose you had the chance to create a new American symbol. It would show what the United States means to you. What would your symbol be? Why?

Write a paragraph to tell about your symbol. Use the steps below to help you.

1 Topic Sentence
Start your paragraph with a topic sentence. Say what your new symbol would be.

2 Detail Sentence
Then write a sentence that gives details of your symbol. Tell what it would look like.

3 Persuasion Sentence
Next, give two reasons why your choice would be a good symbol of the United States.

4 Closing Sentence
Finish your paragraph with a closing sentence. Sum up your main points.

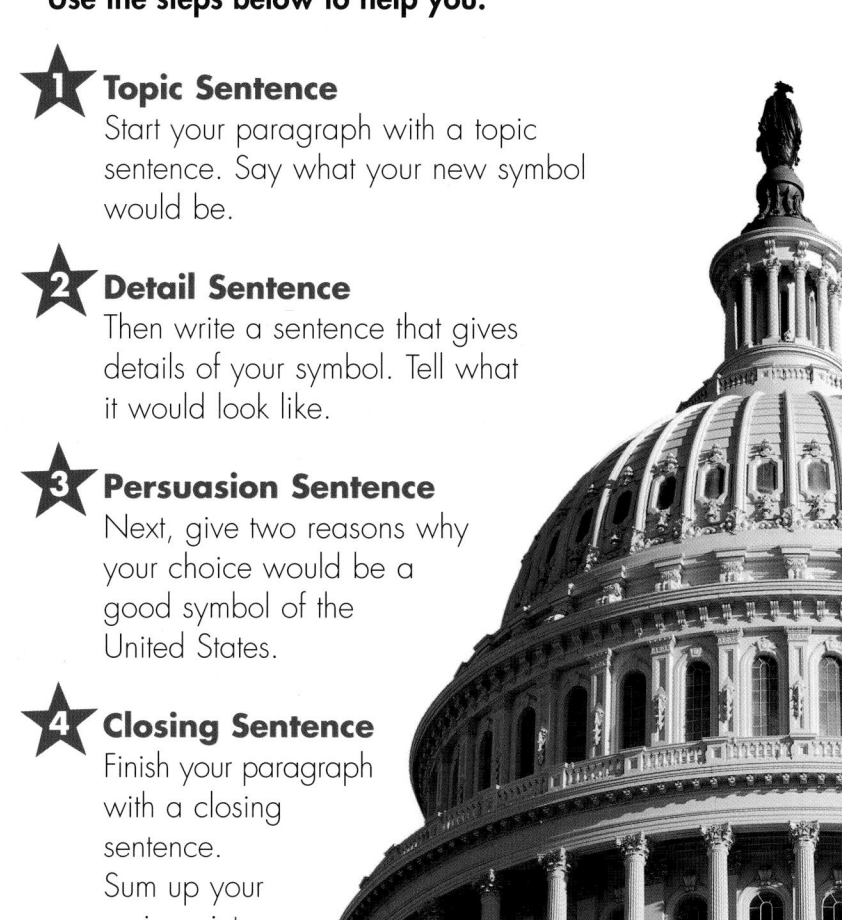

The Star-Spangled

The flag is not the only symbol of our country. We have a national anthem too. It is a song called "The Star-Spangled Banner." Its words are powerful.

The song tells about an important event in American history. It was written during the War of 1812. That was a war between England and the United States.

History in a Song

During the war, the British wanted to take over Baltimore, Maryland. First they had to get past Fort McHenry. This fort was near the harbor. It protected the city.

One night, a battle began. British ships attacked the fort. The fighting was terrible. The battle lasted all day and all night.

Under Attack. ▶ In 1814, British ships attacked Fort McHenry. The battle raged through the night.

◀ **Seeing Stars.** In the morning, Francis Scott Key saw the flag above the fort. He knew the Americans had won.

Banner

The Dawn's Early Light

A man named Francis Scott Key watched the battle. He worried that the Americans might lose. But their flag was still flying the next day. The Americans had won!

Key wrote a poem about the battle. It was printed. Later, it was set to music. In 1932, the song became our national anthem.

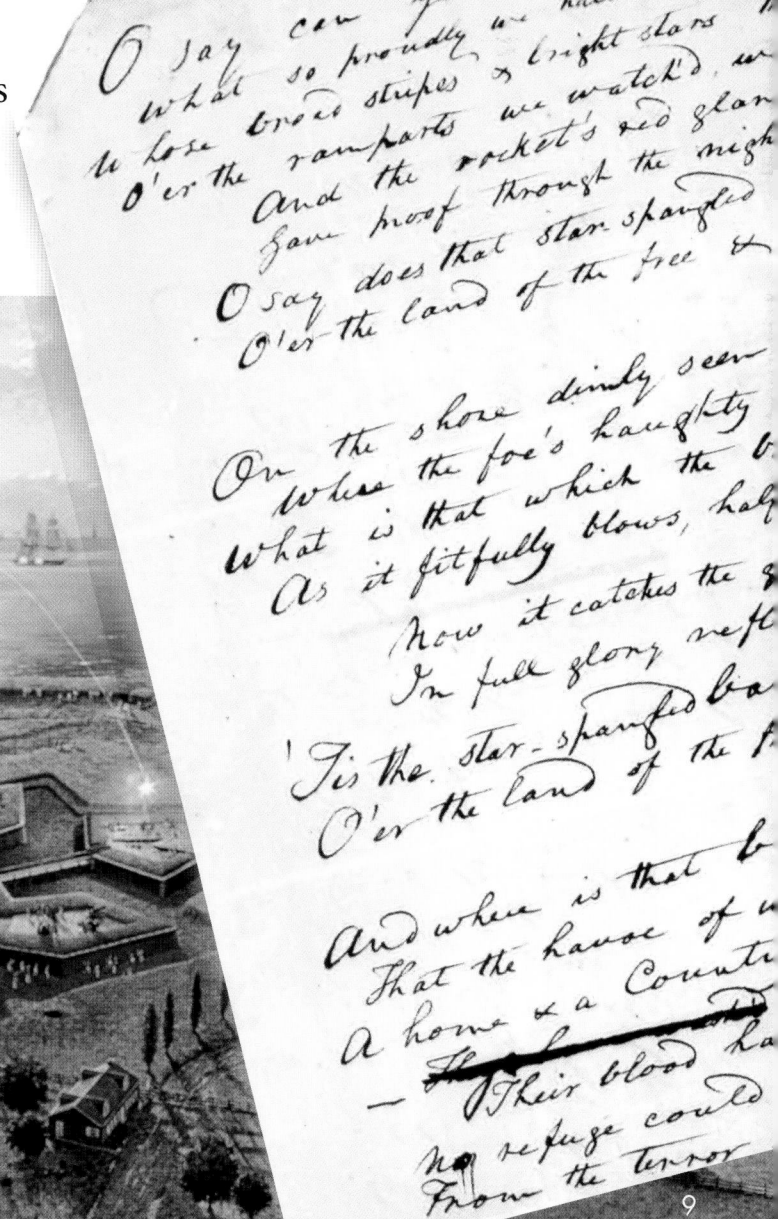

From Poem to Anthem. Francis Scott Key wrote this draft of "The Star-Spangled Banner" in 1814. Congress made the song our national anthem in 1932.

Saving the Stars

The flag that flew above Fort McHenry became famous. But over time, the flag aged. Its fabric grew thin. The flag had holes and rips.

A Banner Project

Luckily, many people decided to save the flag. They began in 1998. They were part of the Star-Spangled Banner Project.

The workers were conservators. They did not want to make the flag look new again. Instead, they cleaned it and made it stronger. They wanted the flag to last a long time.

Years of Work

Work on the famous flag was done at the Smithsonian Institution. It is in Washington, D.C.

The first step was to study the flag. Workers then made a plan. In some places, they had to cut off old stitches.

Next, they cleaned the flag. They dabbed the fabric with sponges. Then they used a special mixture to remove specks of dirt. Finally, they sewed material onto the back of the flag. This made the fabric stronger.

The Future of the Flag

Saving the flag took a lot of time and skill. Yet the years of work paid off. The famous flag was saved!

Soon it will hang in the National Museum of American History. People will enjoy the Star-Spangled Banner for many years to come.

Careful Cuts.
A worker gets ready to cut stitches off the flag. This was one of the steps in saving the flag.

Saving the Past.

The Star–Spangled Banner is over 200 years old. It bears the scars and tears of its long history.

The U.S. Flag

What did you learn about the U.S. flag? Answer these questions to find out.

1 Why did people in Arizona make a "human flag"?

2 What did the Continental Congress decide about the flag?

3 Why has the number of stars and stripes on the flag changed?

4 What event does the national anthem describe?

5 How have people saved the Star-Spangled Banner?